FOUR COLOURS PRODUCTIONS PRESENTS:

Wiigwaas Miinawaa Nichiiwak
Birchbark And Storm

Story & Concept by:
Brita Brookes

Translation by:
Albert Owl
Sagamok FN

Illustration by:
Rachel Mae Butzin

©Copyright. All rights reserved except artwork. Brita Brookes and FOUR Colours Productions. 2011.
©Copyright 2011 Rachel Butzin artwork and character designs, all rights reserved. Used under license.
Reproduction in part or in whole of this work prohibited.

Niizh gaazhagehnsak ayaa'ok.
There are two kittens.

Wiigwaas miinawaa Nichiiwak izhinikaazowag.
Birchbark and Storm are their names.

Sayenh miinawaa shiime ndiyook.
They are brother and sister.

Maamaa daa miinzasaan minagzhidenoon.
Mother's fur is warm.

Wiigwaas makaadewazi
miinawaa waabishkizaa.
Birchbark is black and white.

Daa miinzasaan gwa naasaab
wiigwaasa mtik.
His fur is like the birch tree.

Nichiiwak waabanaawzi.
Storm is gray.

Daa miinzasaan gwa naasaab gchi
zaagigaan ek nchi nichiiwak.
Her fur is like the stormy sea.

Gtigaaning Nichiiwak iyaa.
Storm is in the garden.

Waaskwanesaan waaseyaanon.
The flowers are bright.

Nichiiwak minaashkowaan aamooyin.
Storm chases a bee.

Aamoo bmi maa'aashi.
Bee is in flight.

Aapji gzhiibsa aamoo.
Bee flies fast.

Bejbiza aamoo.
Bee flies slow.

Aamoo gii noogbizha Nichiiwak ojaanzhing.
Bee lands on Storm's nose.

Nichiiwak gii noondaawgzi "oh kaawiin!"
Storm yells "oh no!"

Nichiiwak gii ni zhaabatoo gitigaaning.
Storm runs through the garden.

Wiigwaas geyiin giin noobnakii.
Birchbark follows along.

Gyiw niizh gaazhagenhsaak bzindmook.
The two kittens listen.

OPiichen naagma.
Red Robin sings a song.

Gchinendam opiichi.
Red Robin is happy.

Opiichi gii ni maajiibsa.
Red Robin flies.

Nichiiwak shpiming naabi.
Storm looks above.

Nichiiwak inaabi shpiming giizhgoong.
Storm looks above to the skies.

Waawaaskwasi giizis.
The sun is shining.

Giizis ozaawizi miinawaa gwetaanaasge.
The sun is yellow and bright.

Gaawaan gnaa aankwadoon maa'aasnoon.
The clouds are hanging.

Waabishkaanoon aankwadoon.
The clouds are white.

Niisiiying Nichiiwak naabi.
Storm looks down.

Mtaakmik aganwaamdaan.
She looks down to the ground.

Nichiiwak kidaa giyaatin,
Storm says loudly,

"Naabin, enigoonsak kina ngooji ayaa'ok!"
"Look, ants are all around!"

Doondmitaa'ok enigoonsak.
The ants are busy.

Gbe-giizhik onakii'ok enigoonsak.
The ants work all day.

Nichiiwak daganwaabimaan enigoonsaan.
Storm watches the ants.

Gaawiin enigoonsak odaminosiiwak.
The ants do not play.

Gchi gitigaan aawan.
The garden is big.

Mii maa gaazhagensak bimosewak.
The kittens walk on.

Shpignoon pakweyaashkon.
The ferns are tall.

Gii ngwaabminaagzi giizis.
The sunlight is gone.

Nchiiwak gii mkowaan biimiskodisiin.
Storm finds a snail.

Biimiskodisii giji pakweyaashkoong ayaa.
The snail is on the fern.

Gchi zhoobiingwena biimiskodisiin mii dash ekdat,
The snail smiles and says,

"Nishin binbwaacheyin, aasnaa miinawaa bibskaabiikaan!"
"Nice to visit. Please return!"

"Enh!" kida Nichiiwak miinawaa
"yes" says Storm and

"Aapiish nikeying gi nizhaa'aang?"
"Which way do we go?"

"Oodi nikeying," kida biimiskodisiin.
"That way," says snail.

"E zhaawshkwaagin waawaaskwanesan ezhi zaakiigin."
"The way the violets grow."

Zhaawshkwandenoon waawaaskwanesan.
The violets are purple.

Pii mino-giizigak mii zaakiigin
e zhaawshkwaandegin waawaaskwanesan.
The violets grow in good weather.

E zhaawshkwaa waawaaskwanesa tegin
mii maa Wiigwaas gaa nizhaat.
Birchbark follows the violets.

Miigwanan Nichiiwak ogiimkowaan.
Storm finds a feather.

Ozaawasi miigwanan.
The feather is brown.

Noodin gii maajii aashmaan miigwanan.
The wind catches the feather.

Bimibatoowak miinawaa gwaashkwaniwak gaazhagensak.
The kittens run and jump.

Wiiji-gwaashkwaniwak gaazhagensak.
The kittens jump together.

Wiigwaas agiimkowaan memengwaasan.
Birchbark finds a butterfly.

Niisaying bmibsaa memengwaan.
The butterfly flies lows.

Niizh gaazhagenhsak ganwaabmaawaan.
The two kittens look.

"Aanii!" kidook gaazhagenhsak.
"Hello!" the two kittens say.

Gwanaajiwi memengwaans.
The butterfly is pretty.

Zhaawshkwazi, mkadewazi miinawaa ozhaawashkozi memengwaan.
Butterfly is purple, black and blue.

Nichiiwak aganwaamdaan da ningwiignan.
Storm looks at his wing.

Waawaaskwajiiaanoon shki ningwiignan.
The wings are shiny and new.

Aapiji go gwa naajwaan gitigaan.
The garden is so beautiful.

Wiigwaas miinawaa Nechiiwak bimibatoowak.
Birchbark and Storm run along.

Jiigi ziibi giin ngaabto'ok.
They stop at a stream.

Bzindamok miinawaa ngamwin noondaanaawaa.
They listen and hear a song.

Bapakine nagamo.
The grasshopper sings a song.

Naazhaabiigan mde iyaan da ningwiignoong.
He has a fiddle in his wing.

Wiigwaas bizindaam miinawaa naaniimi.
Birchbark listens and dances.

Nichiiwak maajii ngamaa.
Storm begins to sing.

Niibna nbiish te ziibiing.
The stream is full of water.

Zhiibaabminaagwat miinawaa dkaagmi nbiish.
The water is cold and clear.

Omakakii gii zaabgwanji nbiing.
A frog pops up from the water.

Gaazhigenhsak zhegwaashniwook segzii'ok.
The kittens jump back in fear.

Omakakii zhigwaashni gaazhagenhsak iyaawaat.

Frog hops to the kittens.

Adoo nagay zhaawshkwaani miinawaa ozaawaandeni.

His skin is green and brown.

Nimaadibi omakakii miinawaa nibwaachwe.

Frog sits and visits.

Ni niisaakiiye giizis.

Now the sun is going down.

Zaagidiwook Nichiiwak miinawaa Wiigwaas.
Storm and Birchbark love each other.

Ngidgaamowook.
They are family.

Maamaawaan maakwenmaawaan.
They think about their mother.

Baayaa naabook.
And they look around to see.

Gaamkana gitigaaning, mdeyaa maamaa.
Mother is across the garden.

Gaawiin waasa ndeyaasiin.
She is not far away.

Wiigwaas miinawaa Nichiiwak waabimaawaan.
Birchbark and Storm see her.

Giikendaanaawaa gaawiin maamdaa dashi niigaanbatowaapan.
They know not to stray.

Gaazhagensak giibskaabii'ok maamaawaan yaanit.
The kittens return to their mother.

Mii geyiin ode enji kowaabmaat.
She is waiting for them in sight.

"Ngi chinendam waabmagwaa nbiibiimak!"
"I am glad to see my babies!"

"Mii sashgwa daa naakshing."
"Soon it will be night."

Gaazhagensak wiipemaawaan maamaawan.

The kittens sleep with their mother.

Ezhi Nwaadgamgizwat gaazhagenhsak abji zaagidook.

They are a loving family.

Giikendaanaawaa wii mna bizwat miinawaa wii bwaa zegzowaat.

They now feel safe and warm.

Aabji gaazhagenhsat minoyaa'ok miinawaa niw maamaawaan...

And so they lived happily ever after...

Mii iw Shwaase.

The End.

FOUR Colours Productions:
An Aboriginal and Non-Aboriginal storytelling collaboration creating learning tools for kids of all colours in all languages. Making it FUN to LEARN and PRESERVE languages.

http://www.four-colours.org

A US/Canada Cultural, Arts & Educational Venture

Brita Brookes:
Brita Brookes is a designer and photographer based in Michigan who travels extensively throughout Ontario. Brita has been taking Ojibwe for two years. Brita is founder of VISION Creative Studios and 4 Colors Productions. Trained with a master's degree in architecture and educated in design and photography at Harvard University, Brita has used her creative vision to work on a wide range of community based arts projects. Brita has taught Design Studios at Lawrence Technological University and Wayne State University and has been a visiting critic at the University of Michigan. With a strong talent for brainstorming and conceptual formation, Brita is a favorite among beginning design students for her ability to teach creative, intuitive, and visualization thought techniques. Brita started FOUR Colours Productions because she continually heard language teachers and elders expressing that there was a lack of materials for schools. www.britabrookesgraphics.com

Albert Owl:
Albert Owl is from Sagamok Anisihnaabek Reserve. Ojibwe is his first language. Albert especially likes the expressions on children's faces when they are learning the language. He first studied writing Oijbwe language while going to Cambrian College in Sudbury then recently obtained his Ojibwe Language Teachers Diploma at Lakehead University in Thunder Bay. Albert Owl has translated other story books such as "The Drum Story" published by Reality Media. Other stories that he has worked on include "Niibaakomh, The Recreation Story and The Dream Catcher Story". Albert is thankful for the gift of language and wants to share this knowledge with all the future generations and his beautiful daughter.

Rachel Mae Dennis:
Rachel Mae is a graduate of Michigan State University. From children's books to comic strips, her artwork is always evolving and changing. Rachel Mae is very proud of her Haudenosaunee and Latino heritage and uses her art as a way to share her culture with the world. As a mother of two beautiful little boys she feels it is very important to promote language preservation to protect native culture for future generations. Rachel has done designs for Rez Dog Clothing Company, the Dia de Muijer Conference at MSU, the MSU Pow Wow of Love, Broken Icon Comics and many other events. Rachel has worked on "Ayana goes Fishing" and "Birchbark and Storm" books and videos for FOUR Colours Productions. Rachel is also working on a new comic book series to be done in anishinaabemowin. Rachel's illustrations have a playfulness, hip attitude and light and also evoke a sense of warmth and love. To see more of Rachel's work you can visit her web page: www.mylittlenative.webs.com

FOUR Colours Productions currently receives no funding from grants, casinos, government entities or universities. We have yet to make a profit. But it's been really fun!

www.ingramcontent.com/pod-product-compliance
Lightning Source LLC
Chambersburg PA
CBHW061751290426
44108CB00028B/2964